Set in Stone

by Lisa Trumbauer

Consultant: Paul R. Baker, Professor Emeritus of History,
New York University

Yellow
Umbrella
Books

Yellow Umbrella Books are published by Red Brick Learning
7825 Telegraph Road, Bloomington, Minnesota 55438
http://www.redbricklearning.com

Editorial Director: Mary Lindeen
Senior Editor: Hollie J. Endres
Senior Designer: Gene Bentdahl
Photo Researcher: Signature Design
Developer: Raindrop Publishing
Consultant: Paul R. Baker, Professor Emeritus of History, New York University
Conversion Assistants: Jenny Marks, Laura Manthe

Library of Congress Cataloging-in-Publication Data
Trumbauer, Lisa, 1963-
   Set in Stone / by Lisa Trumbauer
      p. cm.
   ISBN 0-7368-5842-3 (hardcover)
   ISBN 0-7368-5272-7 (softcover)
   1. Monuments—United States—Juvenile literature. 2. Presidents—Monuments—United States—
Juvenile literature. I. Title. II. Series.
   E159.T799 2005
   731'.76'0973—dc22
                                             2005015660

Photo Credits:
Cover: Corbis; Title Page: Michael T. Sedam/Corbis; Page 2: James Randklev/Corbis; Page 3:
Corbis; Page 4: Richard Cummins/Corbis; Page 5: Corel; Page 6: Mark E. Gibson/Corbis;
Page 7: Joseph Sohm/Corbis; Page 8: Kevin Fleming/Corbis; Pages 9 and 10: Corel; Page 11:
Catherine Karnow/Corbis; Page 12: Corbis; Page 13: AP/Wide World Photos; Page 14: Tom
Bean/Corbis; Page 15: Corel

1 2 3 4 5 6 11 10 09 08 07 06

Table of Contents

Earth's History

The history of Earth is set in stone. Tall mountains show how Earth was formed and has changed.

These canyon walls are made of stone. They show the history of a river and the land. See the layers of rock? They show how the Colorado River carved out the Grand Canyon over millions of years.

America's History

The history of people can be found in stone, too. These houses were built in the stone of a cliff in New Mexico. Native Americans once lived here.

The ancestral Pueblo, or Anasazi, built homes out of stone, too. These stone dwellings show the history of a community from long ago. The cliff walls protected the homes from the weather.

Plymouth Rock is in Massachusetts. It reminds us of the history of one of the first groups of English settlers to come to America, the Pilgrims.

The Alamo is in San Antonio, Texas. This is where a famous battle took place between Texas and Mexico in 1836. Davy Crockett fought and died here.

Honoring the Presidents

Washington, D.C., has many stone structures. They help us remember America's history and the people who helped form the United States.

This tall structure is the Washington **Monument**. It **honors** America's first president, George Washington. Made of **marble**, it stands over 550 feet (168 meters) tall.

Thomas Jefferson was the country's third president. He helped write the Declaration of Independence. This marble building honors him.

Abraham Lincoln was president during the Civil War. His marble statue in the Lincoln **Memorial** is nearly 20 feet (6.1 meters) tall.

Mountain Memorials

The faces of Washington, Jefferson, and Lincoln also appear on a mountain. Along with President Theodore Roosevelt, they have been carved on Mount Rushmore, in South Dakota.

Each of the **granite** heads on Mount Rushmore is about 60 feet (18.3 meters) tall. Workers started to make the monument in 1927. They finished in 1942, 15 years later.

Another historical figure is being created in stone near Mount Rushmore. Crazy Horse was a Sioux chief. He fought for Native American **rights**.

Workers are carving Crazy Horse's image into the side of a mountain. The Crazy Horse Memorial and others like it are all symbols of America that have been set in stone.

Glossary

granite—a hard stone, used to make buildings

honor—to show appreciation or respect for someone

marble—a stone that can be polished, and is used to make buildings and statues

memorial—something that is built or an event that is planned to help remember a person or a historical happening

rights—things that people should be allowed to do, such as choosing a place to live or voting

Index

Word Count: 356
Early-Intervention Level: K